YACOB & TOMAS

"I am acting in accordance with the will of the Almighty Creator: by defending myself against the Jew, I am fighting for the work of the Lord."

Adolf Hitler

"If I am not doing the works of my Father, then do not believe me; but if I do them, even though you do not believe me, believe the works, that you may know and understand that the Father is in me and I am in the Father."

Jesus the Christ

EVIL: **Confronting** our Inner Hitler

© 2016 - Brian John Karcher / Yacob & Tomas

All rights reserved. No part of this book may be used or reproduced by any means, graphic, electronic, or mechanical, including photocopying, recording, taping or by any information storage retrieval system without the written permission of the publisher except in the case of brief quotationsembodied in critical articles and reviews.

Infomation / Media:

Yacob & Tomas Worldwide
tbgilman@gmail.com

ISBN 978-0-9965924-6-8 - *hardcover*
ISBN 978-0-9965924-7-5 - *softcover*
ISBN 978-0-9970008-0-1 - *ebook*

Book Design - www.timmyroland.com
Illustration of Lewis & Simone - Linda S. Yenser

for Lewis & Simone,

*my Grandparents who survived Hitler's war
to become the kindest, most loving people.*

*Wedding in Belgium
June 15, 1946*

Table of Contents

Foreword - *T. B. Gilman* i

Introduction iv

Who Was Hitler?

    Deconstructing Mein Kampf 2
    Struggle for Beauty 6
    Struggle to Remove Oppression 9
    Struggle for National Unification 12
    Struggle to Remove Terror 14

What Was Hitler's Message?

    Appealing to the Masses 19
    Promising Utopia to Everyone 22
    Promoting Isolationism as Strength 27

What Was Hitler's Faith?

    The German Jesus 30
    The Political Gospel 32
    The Nazi Bible 35

Confronting Evil

    What is Evil? 39
    The Evil of Exclusion 40
    The Evil of Ideological Conversion 41
    The Evil of Sacred Separation 42
    The Evil of Piety Without Mercy 44
    The Evil of Double Standards 45
    The Evil of Religious Pride 46

The Evil of Violence	48

Lament & Hope

Living Together	52
Resisting Evil	53
Forgiving Our Enemies	55

References   59

FOREWORD

God appeared to Solomon that very night and said, "I accept your prayer; yes, I have chosen this place as a temple for sacrifice, a house of worship. If I ever shut off the supply of rain from the skies or order the locusts to eat the crops or send a plague on my people, and my people, my God-defined people, respond by humbling themselves, praying, seeking my presence, and turning their backs on their wicked lives, I'll be there ready for you: I'll listen from heaven, forgive their sins, and restore their land to health."

2 Chronicles 7:12-14 The Message

It is with clarity and a wide range of emotions that I recall the moment when the announcement invaded our living room letting the world know that Rev. Martin Luther King Jr. has been gunned down as he stood on the balcony of Room 306 at the Lorraine Motel in Memphis in the spring of 1968.

Having just purchased our first portable, black and white, television the reality that we could know so quickly and with such raw emotion the evil actions taking place in our nation was amazing. The thought that someone would be killed simply because he "had a dream" . . . that he stood for justice and peace for not only African Americans, but for all people, was hard for me to understand.

EVIL

However by far the most sobering, the most unsettleing and serious jolt to my world that day was the *response* of many of the people in my world regarding Dr. King's death.

When the news broke we had guests in our home . . . long-time family friends and leaders of our local church. With Martin's death that day there were many in my Christian community that breathed a sigh of relief . . . "we no longer have to worry about him".

In my young mind their relief stopped just a few paces short of rejoicing. I simply could not reconcile this apparent justification of death, oppression and division coming from people of faith—people I knew and trusted with the Jesus that, even at such a young age, I had come to know and had committed to follow.

Thus began my quest to understand, first and foremost for myself, the roots of racism, the roots of injustice, the seedbed in which evil not only takes root but THRIVES. The role that our view and understanding of God, God's character, and the role religion plays in the choices that we make in my relationship with others . . . the choices that my faith community makes in relationships with those around us . . . the choices that my nation makes in relationship to other nations.

The choices we make create environments . . . are we creating the kind of environments in which good takes root *or* in which evil takes root.

What does it mean Jesus mean when He says, "overcome evil with good"?

These questions regarding the very construct of evil are what this book, by my friend and colleague Brian John Karcher, explore through the backdrop of the infamous Nazi leader, Adolf Hitler and the evil he unleashed on the world.

History has been quick to scapegoat on Hitler, making him not only the poster boy for evil but and also, in many people's minds, Lucifer himself.

Confronting our Inner Hitler

Reality is quite different. Hitler was not born evil. Hitler was raised and shaped in a Christian culture—in the very land of Germany where Luther sparked the Reformation. Hitler, for a plethora of reasons, was seduced. Hitler became an evildoer.

There is much for us to learn from the life of the Fuhrer as there is a bit of Hitler in us all and certainly the potential to follow and become doers of evil ourselves.

God's word to Solomon regarding the Jewish people suggests that *humility* is the first foundation stone on which restoration, reconciliation, and the healing of the people and the land is based.

If my people will humble THEMSELVES . . .
If my people who are Christian will humble themselves . . .
If my people who are Muslim will humble themselves . . .
If my people who are Jewish will humble themselves . . .

God says . . . "Then will I . . . "

We would be wise to humble ourselves . . . to each take a fresh look at the texts, that we each hold dear, through the eyes of Jesus.

Humanity will be humbled one way or another . . . wisdom would be to humble ourselves, regardless of how uncomfortable we feel as the process of "being humbled" will be much more painful.

As you read this book refrain from looking at others . . . instead hold the mirror and gaze at yourself . . . Indeed, evil laps at the shoreline of all our hearts.

T. B. Gilman
Follower of Jesus

INTRODUCTION

The little girl screams, startling the Nazi officer about to arrest her brother because he had worn a Belgian flag on his coat. This illegal act warranted a visit from the infamous German occupiers. Seeing the girl, the officer changes his mind. He does not arrest the girl's brother for some unknown reason. Later the little girl screams again, this time because her mother is being taken away. Slapping a Nazi officer happens to be a worse offense than wearing the Belgian flag. Having already lost her father to starvation, the girl enters an orphanage weighing only 48 pounds. She is 13 years old.

A few years later, in 1944, a young man barely 18 years old leaves his quiet American country life in Ohio as he is drafted into the Army. Like so many young men, he is transported from the fields of America into the Second World War. He serves as a Howitzer tank driver in the 747th Field Artillery. Later he would become a truck driver and a chauffeur for an army colonel.

As Hitler waged war to the bitter end and waves of bombs fell on Belgium, this girl and the young man met by chance at a church in Belgium. They could not speak each other's language, so they communicated by tediously translating each word in a dictionary. With the war raging around them, these teenagers fell in love. Millions upon millions of souls never left the terror of that war. By the grace of God, these two not only survived, but became newlyweds less than two years later. In a dark, cold bunker in Germany, Hitler committed suicide—alone and defeated. In a small Belgium church, my Grandparents got married. They married three times in fact, to satisfy the chaotic legal requirements of the time, and as my Grandfather used to joke, just to be sure their marriage was real and so that he could never escape.

What can anyone do in the face of terror? What difference could two teenagers make in a world filled with evil? The answer is as deep as it is obvious—we can humble ourselves and choose to love. We can resist oppression out of love for family and love for country. Love is what drives out fear. Love is how we fight terror. Love is the ageless power that never stops growing. Love is the power that is instantly available and yet takes a lifetime to learn.

And yet another power grows alongside love. Within each of us, evil lurks as well. Why did no one stop Hitler? Could it be that so few people confronted Hitler because so few were willing to confront the Hitler in themselves? Could it be that too many loved what Hitler loved?

Before I begin my examination of Hitler and my ruminations about evil, I wish to share a brief comment about the nature and purpose of this short book. The topic of Hitler and the Nazis is controversial to say the least. The complex topic is also worthy of exhaustive research. My purpose is neither. I write not to stir up controversy in you nor to provide you with a detailed historical account of the perfect storm of politics, religion and culture that occurred in Germany after the First World War. If you wish to read such accounts, I suggest the work of the brilliantly meticulous Ian Kershaw. Four of Kershaw's books comprise 3,782 pages: *Hitler: 1889-1936 Hubris, Hitler: 1936-1945 Nemesis, The Coming of the Third Reich,* and *Hitler: A Biography.* Additionally, I provide a short list of references at the end of my book for those who want to go deeper. My purpose is straightforward—discussion. I begin the discussion by taking an introductory look at Hitler's infamous book, entitled Mein Kampf. Then I share my brief thoughts on the topic of evil. My intention in this short work is to cause you, and myself, to look into our own hearts and

Confronting our Inner Hitler

to spark talking points for further conversations. In all this, I hope to raise more questions than answers. To that end, I have intentionally used brevity to leave you asking more questions.

CONFRONTING OUR INNER HITLER

BRIAN JOHN **KARCHER**

YACOB & TOMAS
WORLDWIDE

Part One

WHO WAS HITLER?

"To be clear: I don't personally believe all rational discourse has ended when Nazis or the Holocaust are invoked. But I'm pleased that people still use Godwin's Law to force one another to argue more thoughtfully. The best way to prevent future holocausts, I believe, is not to forbear from Holocaust comparisons; instead, it's to make sure that those comparisons are meaningful and substantive." [1]

Mike Godwin, Washington Post

Godwin's law is an internet adage asserting that "as an online discussion grows longer, the probability of a comparison involving Nazis or Hitler approaches 100 percent".[1] Often such a comparison immediately ends the discussion. I find this an intellectual tragedy that is hindering our understanding of who Hitler was and how his war machine went off the rails. It would seem that Mr. Godwin, the inventor of Godwin's Law about Hitler comparisons on the internet, agrees, at least in part. He recently wrote an article for the Washington Post saying such comparisons are not always inappropriate, and do not necessarily need to end the conversation. In fact, I find that understanding Hitler and his movement not only begins a new conversation, but radically deepens many thoughtful discourses.

Rather than comparing a specific person to Hitler or pointing out the evils of Nazism, as so many books and people have done before, I strive to gain some understanding of Hitler and his movement. We know how it all ended. But how did such mass evil begin?

By examining the man up close, I believe we can then correctly confront the Hitler in us all. I do this by venturing into the mind of Hitler as expressed in his signature writing, *Mein Kampf*. In doing so, I am not directly comparing or contrasting any person or nation or political party to Hitler. I seek to examine Hitler's own thinking. Then I look for examples of Hitler's thinking in myself, my country and my religion. While we readily distance ourselves from Hitler, I can't help but ask, are we so different? Was there any humanity in the man called Hitler to which we could relate? Hitler is the face of evil, but do we understand that evil?

Regardless of how Hitler ended up, he began as a human being with a very human struggle. *Mein Kampf* in fact means My Struggle. Could the way Hitler handled his struggle be a contributor to the monster he became? When we examine Hitler's thoughts, we may see commonalities in his humanity with ourselves. This does not mean we will become the monster Hitler became. It does mean we should seriously question the path we are taking. Perhaps by seeing some of Hitler's evil in ourselves, and by confronting that evil, we just might make this world a bit more peaceful, hopeful and good.

Deconstructing Mein Kampf

To understand Hitler, I begin with examining his flagship book, entitled *Mein Kampf*. There is much to learn about the man from his writing. For example, typically, other people write the Foreword or Preface components of a book, as endorsements leading to credibility and interest in the book. Such is not the case for *Mein Kampf*. Hitler wrote his own Foreword and his own Preface. This sets an ominous tone for what follows. As such, many people have been too afraid to read Hitler's work. The book has in fact been out of print in Germany since his death on April 30, 1945.

Confronting our Inner Hitler

Seventy years later, however, in 2016, the German Institute for Contemporary History republished a much-annotated version of Hitler's book to serve as a subject of study and to correct many of Hitler's mistaken ideas.[2] The book was written between 1924 and 1926 in two volumes, much of which was written during Hitler's time in jail.[3]

Taking the time to read *Mein Kampf* is quite enlightening. The general themes of the early chapters are about Hitler's family life, especially his struggle with his father's will for Hitler to give up studying architecture and become a civil servant. At times Hitler sounds like a typical teenager arguing with his father about his future occupational choices. Hitler then quickly moves on to the bulk of the book where he expresses his political and pseudo-religious views of the condition of the German people, what caused their condition, and how to restore their country to greatness.

One fascinating part of my preparation for writing this book was to send the text of *Mein Kampf* through various word counters. Exposing the most often repeated words in Hitler's writing reveals the topics he was most concerned with. Overall, the book repeats nine words most often: people, national, German, state, movement, party, world, struggle, and existence. That, in a nutshell, is what Hitler and his movement wanted—they were struggling to rebuild the nation of Germany in a time of world-wide struggle for existence. They were nationalists who looked for unifying power and got caught up in racism.

From the first page of *Mein Kampf*, this purpose is made clear. Hitler intends to outline the goals and development of what he calls "the movement". Throughout the book, we can see the red flags of a man creating a personality cult around himself, with great desire to build up followers who would believe in his movement. From the start, Hitler paints himself, not as the dictator of a new government, but as the face of a new movement.

The well-documented fact about Hitler is of course his blaming of the Jews for the ills that had befallen his beloved

German nation. This theme of racism is obvious right away. Hitler writes in reaction to what he calls "legendary fabrications that the Jewish press has circulated about me."[5] *Mein Kampf* however, reveals that the motivation of Hitler and his movement goes deeper than racism.

The backstory for *Mein Kampf* is perhaps just as important as the writing itself. On June 28, 1919, Germany signed the Treaty of Versailles, officially ending the First World War.[16] The treaty took six months of negotiating and was a surrender by Germany to the United States and the other Allied countries. The treaty contains numerous constraints and restrictions aimed at punishing Germany. Among the hundreds of articles, the treaty called for territorial changes, military mandates, massive reparations and the establishment of international authorities such as the League of Nations.

The treaty brought peace, but not everyone was satisfied with such peace. Germany had been singled out as the scapegoat of the treaty. This uneasy feeling of having gone too far in punishing Germany was present even among the Allied nations. British officials, for example, went on record saying the treaty is "greedy and vindictive". Germany of course was not happy with this treaty, which went way too far in the minds of many Germans. The elected head of the German government, Philipp Scheidemann, resigned rather than sign the treaty, and passionately declared the treaty as "murderous" and "unacceptable".[16] The Germans now found themselves in a surreal situation. They had suffered devastating casualties, world-wide humiliation, and now had to face massive reparations meant to punish the nation of Germany for the sins of their leaders.

Soon after the treaty was signed, Adolph Hitler became so agitated with the situation in Germany that he helped lead a rogue band of revolutionists to take back their country. Hitler was highly disturbed by what he and many other Germans saw as the world's unfair treatment of Germany. The people in this movement saw their German government as weak and apologetic, because the government had surrendered to what

Confronting our Inner Hitler

many deemed as excessive punishment.

Hitler expresses this deep distress in *Mein Kampf*, repeatedly railing against the press, against Communism, against the League of Nations and against numerous ideologies: Christian Socialism, Democratic Socialism, and Marxist Socialism. These themes blur together in rant after rant. It is not clear to me that Hitler understood all these political constructs, and I myself do not have a good enough grasp of the constructs to explain whether Hitler is right or wrong. What is clear to me is that Hitler was dissatisfied with the post-war situation of Germany and was strongly opposed to any form of socialism. Hitler and his movement were steeped in nationalism, imperialism and militant power-mongering. It is no surprise then that Hitler deeply admired the fascist regime in Italy and borrowed the Roman salute to unite his followers. Hitler turned "Hail Ceasar" in to "Hail Hitler".

Hitler's writing reveals that he fears the extermination of the German people at the hands of his enemies—the external enemies of the Allied nations lead by the United States and the League of Nations, and the internal enemies of a status quo government and various socialist ideologies. He feels persecuted by the press, by the world, and by his own government. He seeks to find a way to respond to terrorists. As time went on Hitler became so agitated that he joined hundreds of others in an armed revolt in a beer hall.

On November 8th 1923, four years after the Treaty of Versailles, approximately two thousand men marched with Hitler and confronted the police in a pub in Munich. Sixteen Nazis and four policemen died. Hitler himself was wounded and sentenced to jail for the uprising, charged with treason. The defeat came to be known as the Beer Hall Putsch.[6] Hitler's revolt and the Nazi party was over. Except that it wasn't.

Alone in a jail cell, with almost no real political experience, Hitler decides to reimagine his Nazi Party revolution. He documents his plans and begins writing his book, *Mein Kampf*. He decides against a violent overthrow of the government by force, for that had simply landed him in jail. Hitler hated the incumbent German government, but also knew that his small band of agitators was too weak to actually confront the government and overthrow it by force. Instead, Hitler sees a different way. He would enter politics legally and advance his movement's cause by stepping into the established system. We know that Hitler was not against using violence when necessary, but he also saw the strategic value of rising to power lawfully. To that end, Hitler put his political ideas on paper in the form of *Mein Kampf*.

Hitler believed that his movement was pure, correct and stronger than ever. The reality was quite different, but Hitler had already grown accustomed to dictating his own reality onto the world. With persuasive, often non-specific but always inspiring words, Hitler paints himself and his country in *Mein Kampf* as the victims, and wins over the judge who kept him in jail. After a 24 day, highly publicized trial, Hitler is released several years before his sentence for treason ends. Hitler emerges from jail as a celebrity-like hero and gains more momentum than ever before.

Hitler's struggle for power begins with his first step out of that jail cell. What was he struggling for? What was he seeking? *Mein Kampf* records at least four themes that begin to provide insight into such complex questions. Hitler struggled to find beauty, to remove oppression, to unite his country, and to rid his country of terrorism.

Struggle for Beauty

> "But when people try to approach these questions with drivel about aesthetics, etc., really only one answer is possible: where the destiny and existence of a people are at stake, all obligation toward beauty ceases. The most unbeautiful thing there can be in human life is and remains the yoke of slavery." [5]
>
> *Adolf Hitler*

Confronting our Inner Hitler

The first theme of Hitler's book that struck me was the struggle for pure beauty. At various times in *Mein Kampf*, Hitler muses on the subject of beauty with an almost love-hate relationship. He seems desperate to find beauty, and if beauty is not possible, destruction is his response. He shares his love for art, painting and architecture with a chip on his shoulder. Hitler express his frustration over two events: his father's direction for Hitler to become a civil servant and Hitler's rejection by the Vienna School of Fine Arts.

He writes about his desire to become an architect, which he saw as an extension of his self-proclaimed painting skills. This struggle to see beauty led him to study in the magnificent city of Vienna, Austria. Hitler loved both painting and architecture, but could not decide between the two paths. Would he become a painter or an architect? Hitler recalls his trip to Vienna with mixed emotions and with a "drop of bitterness". He loved the Opera and recalls gazing at the magnificent buildings:

> *"For hours I could stand in front of the Opera, for hours I could gaze at the Parliament; the whole Ring Boulevard seemed to me like an enchantment out of The Thousand-and-One-Nights."* [5]
>
> *Adolf Hitler*

Hitler's trip to Vienna was during a turbulent time of his life. His father had already passed away and his mother was dying of breast cancer. He had just recently dropped out of high school and now takes his inheritance money to travel to Vienna. He applies to study art at the prestigious Vienna Academy of Fine Arts.

Hitler was highly confident that the school would fall in love with his painting abilities. But after a two day entrance exam, the professors were not impressed. His application to art school was rejected, and by a Jewish professor no less. It was noted on his application that he might want to try architecture classes. This struck Hitler like what he calls a "bolt from the blue". He wondered the city aimlessly, filled with the depression of rejection. The thought entered Hitler's mind to take the school's suggestion to study architecture, but he could not pursue this path because he did not have a high school diploma. And so, after his application to art school in Vienna was rejected, Hitler returned home to his dying mother with a cloud of depression swirling around him. Hitler's quest for beauty had failed miserably.

Hitler's writing reveals that his struggle to see beauty in the world had a twisted side. From an early age, he garnered a tremendous love for the glory of war. Hitler saw war as beautiful. He seemed to live and breathe with the glory of battle. While other boys played in the park, Hitler stayed at home, enthralled by his father's library. He come across various military books, such as one book detailing the history of Franco-German War. These war books became his favorite reading material. In Hitler's imagination, he played out the great heroic struggles. The glory of war became what he calls his "greatest inner experience". From his youth, he became more and more enthusiastic about everything that was in any way connected with war, soldiers, and battle.

In the end, Hitler's struggle for beauty becomes delusional, as he attributes the source of all beauty to one race of people, the German people. He writes: "Everything we admire on this earth today--science and art, technology and inventions--is only the creative product of a few peoples and originally perhaps of one race." Hitler sees the German people not only as the source of all beauty, but the defenders of such beauty. In Hitler's mind, the beauty of the earth lives and dies with the German people. On them depends the existence of all cultures and the existence of the entire civilized word. If the Germans perish, beauty ceases to exist. Thus, in Hitler's mind, the war reparations after the First World War were particularly grievous. The German people must become strong to fight against the unjust treaty. Instead of war criminals, the German people are, to Hitler, the great protectors of civil society.

In this then, we see the first of the numerous components of evil along the path Hitler chose. Hitler sought beauty and if such beauty was not possible, then his desire was to

Confronting our Inner Hitler

destroy it all. The struggle to create, defend and protect all the beauty in the world is a struggle doomed right from the start, for what man or woman or country can claim such a grand responsibility? How do we respond to a world where beauty is elusive? What do we do when we are rejected by the world for our greatest passion? Can we appreciate the glimpses of beauty the world affords us? Is the existence of all beauty bound up in one race? Can we see the beauty of other races and cultures?

Struggle to Remove Oppression

> *"As long as my father's intention of making me a civil servant encountered only my theoretical distaste for the profession, the conflict was bearable. Thus far, I had to some extent been able to keep my private opinions to myself; I did not always have to contradict him immediately. My own firm determination never to become a civil servant sufficed to give me complete inner peace. And this decision in me was immutable. The problem became more difficult when I developed a plan of my own in opposition to my father's. And this occurred at the early age of twelve."*[5]
>
> *Adolf Hitler*

Right away, *Mein Kampf* makes one theme clear, with grand irony: oppression will not be tolerated. Hitler refuses to be oppressed, and shares a rather ordinary struggle—he hated his father's will for him to become a civil servant. Hitler writes of his "immutable opposition" to his father's desire for him to be a civil servant. Hitler would *not* work for the government. He writes that he experienced terrible consequences as he opposed his father, without describing the details of those consequences.

Some have mused that Hitler's evil is rooted in this struggle with his father, and his father's subsequent abusive treatment. Whatever the case, the struggle with his father's oppression was most impactful. Hitler wanted to be an artist, struggling against his father's will. At times, Hitler's writing reads like a typical teenager's diary.

The struggle of a young boy against his father's will continued throughout Hitler's youth. As he grew older, he fought against forces he deemed oppressive to him and his country. One of these repeated sources of oppression Hitler writes about is the press, which he greatly disliked. To Hitler, the press was a source of division and was destroying the German nation. He saw the press as a voice for pacifism, and thus was weakening the military defense and undermining the greatness of Germany:

> "But what food did the German press of the pre-War period dish out to the people? Was it not the worst poison that can even be imagined? Wasn't the worst kind of pacifism injected into the heart of our people at a time when the rest of the world was preparing to throttle Germany, slowly but surely? Even in peacetime didn't the press inspire the minds of the people with doubt in the right of their own state, thus from the outset limiting them in the choice of means for its defense? Was it not the German press which knew how to make the absurdity of 'Western democracy' palatable to our people until finally, ensnared by all the enthusiastic tirades, they thought they could entrust their future to a League of Nations?" [5]
>
> *Adolf Hitler*

In my reading of *Mein Kampf*, it seems to me that hiding behind the press and the Jews was another of Hitler's great oppressors of the nation: liberalism. Hitler saw liberalism as an enemy hiding behind every corner. To Hitler, liberalism was evil. He writes with disdain about the liberal ideas of the Jews and their progressive ideas oppressing the nation:

> "But even more: all at once the Jew also becomes liberal and begins to rave about the necessary progress of mankind. Slowly he makes himself the spokesman of a new era."[5]
>
> *Adolf Hitler*

Confronting our Inner Hitler

This idea of removing the oppression of liberalism takes form in Hitler's writing when he writes about the various expressions of socialism. Hitler rants over and over about the evil he sees in Communism, Marxism and the Christian and Social Democratic parties. In Hitler's mind these socialist-based political constructs were not only a threat to Germany, but a threat to all humanity. Hitler and his movement promoted nationalism. Here is one example from the early chapters:

> *"Up to that time I had known the Social Democratic Party only as an onlooker at a few mass demonstrations, without possessing even the slightest insight into the mentality of its adherents or the nature of its doctrine; but now, at one stroke, I came into contact with the products of its education and 'philosophy.' And in a few months I obtained what might otherwise have required decades: an understanding of a pestilential whore, cloaking herself as social virtue and brotherly love, from which I hope humanity will rid this earth with the greatest dispatch, since otherwise the earth might well become rid of humanity."*[5]
>
> *Adolf Hitler*

In the middle chapters of *Mein Kampf,* Hitler weaves the thoughts about these various oppressors together into one narrative. He sees the liberal press and the masterful Jews and the Social Democrats as great enemies of the German flag. In Hitler's mind these great oppressors were soiling the "black, red and gold" colors on their flag. They were not true to the great German spirit of yesteryear. He longed to return to the old days when he supposed that Germans were "honest souls".

I feel the need to pause here. What is the evil in what Hitler wrote in these sections of his book? I do not see the disdain for liberalism as evil, any more than disdain for conservatism is evil. These are merely differing political and social viewpoints. Conservatives need the values liberalists bring to the table just as much as liberals need conservative values. And we all need the level-headedness of the moderates.

The evil here is in the fear—fear that those we disagree are taking over the country and destroying it; fear that if the *other* party rules our country then humanity is lost. The evil lies in fearfully pinning the problems of Germany on one specific people, the Jews, and on one specific ideology, socialism, and then passionately trying to eliminate this oppression. Disagreement is not evil; destruction is evil.

Hitler's evil rampage began with a mass stirring of the feeling of being oppressed. Hitler pointed out both real and imaginary oppressors all with the aim of creating a revolution. His movement desired to remove these self-identified sources of oppression and to restore the German flag, the "black, red and gold", to glory.

The struggle to remove oppression is a good struggle. Is it always necessary? Can we know so clearly who is doing the oppressing? Do we respond to oppression by destroying the oppressor? Might we all have a hand in causing the oppression or is all oppression caused by one source? Are we aware of how we are oppressing the people around us?

Struggle for National Unification

> *"German-Austria must return to the great German mother country, and not because of any economic considerations. No, and again no: even if such a union were unimportant from an economic point of view; yes, even if it were harmful, it must nevertheless take place. One blood demands one Reich. Never will the German nation possess the moral right to engage in colonial politics until, at least, it embraces its own sons within a single state."* [5]
>
> *Adolf Hitler*

Any reader of *Mein Kampf* immediately notices another major theme—Hitler's desire to unite his country. He hated division, and saw any sacrifice worth the price of unification. Right from the start, we see the struggle to form a united

Confronting our Inner Hitler

people.

Hitler repeats his desire for uniting his beloved country, almost as a young child longs for his father and mother to reunite. Perhaps the early loss of his own mother and father weighed heavily in the back of Hitler's mind? To Hitler, the uniting of Germany and Austria was a supreme imperative, regardless of any consequences.

Hitler repeatedly shares his frustrations with the current government's failure to unite the country. He sees the government as weak, lacking the courage and stamina to forge one German nation. From an early age, Hitler gained this passion for hating the government. He speaks glowingly about his anti-establishment teachers:

> *"This teacher made history my favorite subject. And indeed, though he had no such intention, it was then that I became a little revolutionary. For who could have studied German history under such a teacher without becoming an enemy of the state which, through its ruling house, exerted so disastrous an influence on the destinies of the nation? And who could retain his loyalty to a dynasty which in past and present betrayed the needs of the German people again and again for shameless private advantage?"* [5]
>
> *Adolf Hitler*

In *Mein Kampf*, when Hitler writes of unity, he writes of "the inner unity of our people's will". He writes of "unity of blood", a racial unity that supposedly has power to create a better society. He deems diversity as an evil plaguing the German people. He thinks that a "herd instinct" is a necessary element for a great nation:

> *"The fundamental racial elements are not only different in different districts, but there are also various elements in the single districts. Beside the Nordic type we find the East-European type, beside the Eastern there is the Dinaric, the Western type intermingling with both, and hybrids among them all. That is a grave drawback for us. Through it the*

EVIL

> *Germans lack that strong herd instinct which arises from unity of blood and saves nations from ruin in dangerous and critical times; because on such occasions small differences disappear, so that a united herd faces the enemy."* [5]
>
> *Adolf Hitler*

This is the evil in the struggle for national unity—Hitler struggled for unity based on uniformity. He sought unity through common blood, ignoring the reality that such uniformity is a destructive force when applied to humanity. For it is human blood that unites human beings. No race or people is superior or inferior to the rest of humanity. Unity sought through uniformity results in dire consequences.

Hitler's voice was loud in those times, and his movement powerful. Still the voice of unity through diversity was not completely silent. For example, the great Spanish cellist, Pablo Casals once said this: "The love of one's country is a splendid thing. But why should love stop at the border?" Casals wrote the music for the United Nations anthem for world peace and recorded his famous Bach Cello Suites from 1936 to 1939. Hitler and his movement raged on however, ignoring the Casals of the world. Perhaps many Germans lost themselves in such music, hoping for the release of the building tension. Alas, history shows that Hitler's ideas of nationalism won over the people.

Can we hear the voices of diversity? Are we willing to embrace those who are different from us? Does not our own human body, composed of numerous different parts, demonstrate what unity looks like? Is not unity through diversity the most powerful form of unity? Do we not find the most about ourselves when we walk in the shoes of those most different from us?

Struggle to Remove Terror

> *"Terror at the place of employment, in the factory, in the meeting hall, and on the occasion of mass demonstrations*

Confronting our Inner Hitler

will always be successful unless opposed by equal terror." [5]

Adolf Hitler

The terror unleashed by the Reich has roots in Hitler's desire to remove terror. Hitler himself did not initially intend to unleash terror, but to remove it. This is the surprising theme I found in *Mein Kampf*--the struggle against terror. Why would the man who unleashed the greatest terror on earth be writing about a struggle to remove terror?

Hitler was afraid of terrorists. His response? Fight terror with terror. It could be said, therefore, that the massive terror invoked by Hitler is matched equally only by his fear. The Third Reich often acted out of a dizzying froth of desire to protect their movement from outside terror. In essence, Hitler and the Reich believed they were the good defenders, the protectors of their nation.

Mein Kampf speaks to this clearly. In addition to a struggle to remove oppression and those who stood in his way, Hitler's writing reveals that he sought to protect the German people. He writes of wanting to protect his country from terrorists:

> *"I have emphasized that in certain circumstances a movement which is meant to win over the hearts of the people must be ready to defend itself with its own forces against terrorist attempts on the part of its adversaries. It has invariably happened in the history of the world that formal State authority has failed to break a reign of terror which was inspired by a Weltanschauung (worldview). It can only be conquered by a new and different Weltanschauung (worldview) whose representatives are quite as audacious and determined."*[5]

Adolf Hitler

Hitler's thoughts here equate to responding to a bully by punching the bully in the face. He seeks to fight terror with terror. Throughout *Mein Kampf*, he writes about physical terror, spiritual terror and psychological terror. At one point he seems infatuated with such thoughts. Terror is a theme woven into *Mein Kampf*. At times it is difficult to discern if Hitler is struggling to remove the terror threat or to create it. He admires those who are able to use terror effectively. When writing of the Communists (the Reds), he writes: "they were determined to use every means to get rid of a movement which did seem dangerous to them. Their most effective method in such cases has at all times been terror or violence." [5]

Here we should be able to see another evil in Hitler's thoughts. He seeks to remove terror with equal or greater terror. He seeks peace through war. Hitler wants a safe place, free of what he sees as the source of terror, for his country. The desire for safety is not evil, but the methods of creating a safe place through equal terror is evil. Such equal-force terror is exactly what Hitler prescribed. How do we respond to terrorists? How do we find peace and safety when violence and war intrude upon us? Do we punch back with equal or greater force? When will the cycle of terror end? Who will be the first to lay down our weapons?

Throughout *Mein Kampf*, I see passion for some of the goals we all want—beauty, freedom, unity and safety. The evil path Hitler chose lies not in these goals, but primarily in the manner in which he sought these goals. Hitler's path was one of placing ultimate value on obtaining his ideals at any cost, convinced he was correct and ignoring any rejection or criticism. Hitler's evil is the struggle to create pure beauty in a world of rejection, the struggle to remove oppression by destroying the oppressor, the struggle to unite people by forceful uniformity, and the struggle to remove terror by the force of terror.

We like to place all the blame for evil on Hitler. Yet it was his following, the mass support of the people and government officials, who bear most of the burden. The Third Reich, influenced by Hitler, became a radicalized force of terror, not at once, but over time.

Chapter Two

WHAT WAS HITLER'S MESSAGE?

"Simplicity and repetition were two key ingredients in his speaking armoury. These revolved around the unvarying essential driving-points of his message: the nationalization of the masses, the reversal of the great 'betrayal' of 1918, the destruction of Germany's internal enemies (above all the 'removal' of the Jews), and material and psychological rebuilding as the prerequisite for external struggle and the attainment of a position of world power. This conception of the path to Germany's 'salvation' and rebirth was already partially devised, at least in embryo, by the date of his letter to Gemlich in September 1919."

Ian Kershaw, Hitler: A Biography

Hitler's message is stained not only with charismatic persuasion, unspecified hope and inspiring images, but also with doubt, fear and elitism. He became the voice of those dissatisfied with the press, with the losses of the First World War, and with the fear of losing the German nation to foreign threats. Hitler voiced the concerns of those furious with the status quo German government. Upon this platform, Hitler built his regime.

In 1931, Hitler's niece commits suicide[7], spiraling Hitler into deep depression. It is this depression from which the Presidential campaigns of Hitler began. Yes, Hitler ran for President of Germany. These campaigns are another surprising element that emerged from my study of Hitler. I had always believed Hitler must have used violence to force his way into office against the will of the people. Nothing could be farther from the truth. While Hitler did indeed come to power forcefully, he did so with the support of tens of millions of votes and massive popularity in a Christianized nation. He gave campaign speeches from churches and spun up slick propaganda tours.

After being jailed for his coup attempt, and then successfully negotiating his release, Hitler decided to come to power by legal means. He learned that the ultimate power he needed to create his grand utopian nation required the willful support of the mass population and the authority of the German military. So he quickly learned the ways of populism. What mattered, Hitler realized, was not his experience but his decisive boldness.

When the First World War ended, the German government was in shambles. The government limped along as an ineffective body, rendered stagnant by constant bickering and a lack of leadership. Hitler aimed to change all that. Hitler would shake up the old guard and ring in a new Germany with decisiveness unmatched by any other politician. Election after election, he gained support, not necessarily for his good ideas or detailed plans, but for his courageous and heroic statements. He took photo after photo smiling with children, laughing with the people and ushering in a new, strong Germany. In photo after photo, Hitler posed in awe-inspiring grandeur, always presenting himself in a powerful light.

In the presidential election held on March 13, 1932, Hitler got over eleven million votes. This was 30% of the total and meant that Hitler came in second to the incumbent President, Paul von Hindenburg. Hindenburg obtained 18,651,497 votes or 49% of the total votes.[8] This result, with neither the current President nor the challenging Hitler winning a majority, meant no one won the election. German law required an absolute majority to win, or over 50%. Therefore, a run-off election became necessary. Hitler jumped at the opportunity with a blitzkrieg election campaign across Germany. And with each

Confronting our Inner Hitler

election, the mystique of Hitler grew more and more popular.

Appealing to the Masses

"The German people were desperate for relief from the tremendous personal suffering brought on by the Great Depression, now two years old. Millions were unemployed, thousands of small businesses had failed, homelessness and starvation were real possibilities for everyone. Civilization itself was unraveling in Berlin where people were fighting in the streets, killing each other in the chaos. But from their elected leaders, the people got nothing but indecision. In ever growing numbers they turned to the decisive man, Adolf Hitler, and his promises of a better future."[7]

The History Place

One infamous political campaign was called "Hitler Over Germany". The title referenced Hitler's airplane trips, where he canvased Germany for dozens of speeches in several weeks. It was in fact, the beginning of Hitler's legal dictatorship rule over Germany. In grand, heart-stopping fashion, Hitler flew into larger and larger crowds, who were frantic to catch a glimpse of their political savoir. The rallies included something for everyone; a smorgasbord of promises, as if bread had dropped from the sky. Hitler's mysticism and decisiveness appealed to millions of Germans, including many among the college-educated and church-going faithful.

Sunday, April 10, 1932—the run-off voting began. Hitler increased about two million votes and grabbed 36% of the total votes. This again was not enough, and Hitler fell to second place. Hindenburg won with 19,359,983 votes, just enough to win decisively with 53% of the vote.[8] Hindenburg was therefore re-elected by an absolute majority. Hitler lost. Hindenburg would serve another seven-year term. Hitler was appealing to the masses, but had not yet secured enough votes to become President. Some thought they had seen the last of Hitler.

EVIL

In spite of the Presidential election loss, Hitler and the Nazi Party continued their campaigns throughout the summer in order to gain seats in the German Parliamentary elections. They knew they could not succeed as rulers of Germany without the support of the German Army or the German industrialists. So the Nazis campaigned in every corner of Germany to put their party in government, riding on the heels of Hitler's popularity. Everyone watched with anticipation and growing anxiety as the country headed into the unknown with an increasingly nervous population and a status-quo incumbent President.

Within months, the German government collapsed and could no longer maintain peace. Violence ensued as Nazi Brownshirts scoured the streets, picking fights with the Communists. The situation was extremely uncertain. The very fabric of German culture was tearing at the seams. Chaos ruled. The Germans desperately sought someone to take control.

July 1932—New elections gave the Nazi Party new life. By now, Hitler was speaking to rallies of up to 100,000 people. Often he would make dramatic entrances, making his audience of supporters wait for minutes on end. Then when he stepped up to the podium, Hitler would pause many more minutes before speaking, letting the tension to build. Hitler had successfully, and legally, built his own personality cult with millions of followers. Whatever doubts people had were cast aside as people adored Hitler's charismatic, decisive spirit and drank in his glorious, nostalgia-soaked promises of hope for a better Germany.

July 31, 1932—the people vote again. The Nazi Party faired about the same as before, with just under 14 million votes and 37% of the total. But by now they had gained 230 seats in the German Parliament, called the Reichstag. The Nazi Party was now the largest and most powerful political force in Germany.

In the next year, in 1933, the German nation reached a boiling point. The people demanded that someone take control. And so, reluctantly, President Hindenburg appointed Hitler as

Confronting our Inner Hitler

Chancellor of the German Nation. This gave Hitler a major role in government decisions and showed the unruly bands of gangs running wild in the streets that their time was up. Hitler was in power now.

President Hindenburg reluctantly agreed to appoint Hitler to Chancellor due to the popularity Hitler and the Nazi Party had with the people, and the need to bring an end to the violence. The streets of Germany were filling with chaos with each passing day, and Hindenburg needed a strong leader to garner the confidence of the people. Hitler celebrated his appointment as Chancellor with a parade, driving through the streets to greet his wildly cheering fans. In the mind of Hitler and in the hearts of his followers, Hitler was already President. It was just a matter of time and their political savior would restore greatness to Germany.

With his new power, Hitler bullied his way further into the German state system, forcefully but legally. He demanded more and more elections to ensure the support of the people. He dissolved the Parliament and setup his own Nazi controlled power structure so that Hitler's decrees would be passed into law unchecked. Now, with money no longer an issue, the Nazis campaigned furiously. Hitler obtained any majority vote he wanted.

March 5, 1933—the last free elections in Germany were held. In spite of all his campaigning, Hitler and the Nazis still lost! After all that had happened, Hitler and his movement did not gain a majority vote in the election. The Nazi Party fell short with only 44 percent of the total vote, just over 17 million.[8] Somehow, the Social Democrats managed to get over 7 million votes, and both the Center Party and the Communists held their own in the election.

By now, Hitler was used to falling short, and he would not accept defeat. With his power as Chancellor and with systematic precision, Hitler and the Nazis began taking over the local governments by force. Traditionally, the local area governments in Germany had been left alone to govern without national control. Hitler put that to an end, sometimes violently replacing the local leaders with Nazi Party officials. Those who opposed Hitler and the Nazis become fewer and fewer. In this way Hitler gerrymandered his way into more power.

The final step in securing Hitler's dictatorship came in just a few weeks, on March 23, 1933. Hitler presents his "Enabling Act". This was Hitler's "Law for Removing the Distress of the People and the Reich." This short legal document was the final piece of the puzzle for removing democracy from Germany and establishing Hitler's dictatorship-style government.

A politician named Otto Wells clashed with Hitler just before te voting on the Enabling Act. Wells was the leader of the Social Democrats. His words ignited fury in Hitler but echo one final plea of resistance throughout the halls of history:

> *"We German Social Democrats pledge ourselves solemnly in this historic hour to the principles of humanity and justice, of freedom and socialism. No enabling act can give you power to destroy ideas which are eternal and indestructible."*[8]
>
> Otto Wells

Hitler's Enabling Act was not opposed by his Nazi-infused government, and was passed by 441 votes yes; 84 votes no. And with that, Hitler's legal dictatorship was born. Millions of his supporters celebrated and breathed a massive sigh of relief. The German people imagined that finally they had a leader to establish Germany's glorious existence once and for all. Others however waited nervously.

Promising Utopia to Everyone

> *"In the Third Reich, every German girl will find a husband! . . . Hitler promised everything from husbands to jobs to world power--and people across Germany believed him. Many who had questioned him in the past were awestruck*

Confronting our Inner Hitler

by Hitler's dynamic speaking and were overwhelmed by the Nazi display of strength and national pride. It contrasted vividly with Germany's depressed state."

> Mark Thomas
> *The Deadliest War: The Story of World War II*

What kind of message has such mass appeal as Hitler's message? Fear is certainly part of the message. Fear alone however does not explain why millions of people voted for Hitler and cheered him on so enthusiastically. What was his message? Hitler understood a basic premise of populism well: to sway masses of people you do not present complicated theories, but grand, simple promises. Hitler knew this and wrote in *Mein Kampf* admiringly about how the Communist revolutionists did just that:

> *"The masses of illiterate Russians were not fired to Communist revolutionary enthusiasm by reading the theories of Karl Marx but by the promises of paradise made to the people by thousands of agitators in the service of an idea."* [5]

In my reading, it seems one such promise of paradise stood at the foundation of Hitler's speeches. That promise is the hope for a new, powerful, glorious nation. Hitler spoke often of how weak and flawed the German government had become. He proposed a "radical elimination of the whole ruling system", and portrayed the existing Reich leaders as betrayers of Germany. Hitler writes in grandiose terms about a complete overhaul of the German government.

> *"In millions of minds the conviction suddenly arose bright and clear that only a radical elimination of the whole ruling system could save Germany."* [5]

Stemming from this fundamental promise of a brand new government and a shiny new united nation, were promises for everyone, young or old. Among these promises were the following... [9]

- **To the middle class,** Hitler promised protection from Communism, and restoration of law and order.

- **To the upper class,** Hitler promised reprisal for the Treaty of Versailles, and the creation of a strong government.

- **To the large industrialists,** Hitler promised suspension of trade unions.

- **To the working class,** Hitler promised jobs and the protection of workers.

- **To ordinary people from the countryside,** Hitler promised an increase in the price of agricultural products.

- **To women,** Hitler promised his new government would have an emphasis on the family and on a moral society.

One of Hitler's most famous speeches, the March 21st 1933 speech delivered in the Garrison Church at Potsdam, reveals Hitler's utopian campaign promises. To Hitler, these were not purely political promises, but rather the right of the German people. The speech, dubbed "The Day of Potsdam" was Hitler's acceptance speech for becoming Chancellor. The speech was accompanied by an elaborate ceremony, designed to ease public concern over Hitler's bullish ways. President Hindenburg, foreign diplomats, the General Staff and many from the old guard were present. The Propaganda Minister, Joseph Goebbels, put on a display for the ages in brilliant color. He presented Hitler in humble fashion, cloaked in statesman glory. Hitler was on his best behavior, respectfully

Confronting our Inner Hitler

shaking the hand of President Hindenburg and speaking with calm dignity and as much humility as he could muster. Hitler payed his respect to the old guard, blending the old Prussian military with the new Nazi Reich.[7]

> "The 'Day of Potsdam' was to represent the start of the new Reich building upon the glories of the old. It was also to denote the forging of the links between the new Germany and the traditions of Prussia. The garrison church in Potsdam, where the main ceremony was to take place, had been founded by the Hohenzollern Kings of Prussia in the early eighteenth century. The church symbolized the bonds between the Prussian military monarchy, the power of the state, and the Protestant religion."
>
> Ian Kershaw, Hitler: A Biography

In this one moment—the speech from a grand old church—the perfect storm of politics, religion and nationalism came together all at once. It was a moment of pride and peace and celebration for the German people. The voices of those who doubted or criticized were drowned out, for the church itself was the stage.

Promoting Isolationism as Strength

Perhaps the most intriguing aspect of *Mein Kampf* to me is the chapter in Volume 2 entitled "The strong is strongest when alone". In this chapter, Hitler promotes the idea that collaboration and coalition building are hindrances to the strong. He expounds on the idea of isolating the country from external relationships.

For example, Hitler writes:

> "It must never be forgotten that nothing really great in this world has ever been achieved through coalitions, but that such achievements have always been due to the triumph of the individual."[5]

EVIL

I find this idea of triumphant individualism to be an extraordinary picture of evil deception, and one that plagues our America today. When Hitler speaks of being alone, he is speaking about two ideas simultaneously. He is saying "Be alone" and "Stay in the Movement" at the same time. This is one of the hallmarks of people who create personality cults around them. After reading Hitler's writing, I find that this is exactly what Hitler did—create a personality cult centered on isolationism. Thus, Hitler became a magical caricature, the face of his movement. Much of the blame for his rise to power then rests in those who followed him and enabled his movement.

To preach such a message of isolationism is what destructive cults preach. I know this because for over twenty years, my life was bound up in a Korean Bible cult. In the cult, we preached isolationism. We always taught that we had the best Bible study, and that we did not need the weak, watered-down ideas of seminary schools or Christian commentaries. We had the truth, we thought. We are stronger alone, we imagined. We do not need collaboration or the nominal teachings of the mainstream Christian churches, we boasted.

At no time however did we think that this meant an individual could survive without the group. This dualistic nature of cultic teaching kept us bound to the movement. We believed we were strong together with our personality cult leader, isolated from the sinful world around us. I see these cultic undertones in Hitler and his movement.

As I read *Mein Kampf*, I find myself recalling my cult life days. I can easily imagine how educated, church-going Germans would be drawn in by Hitler's deceptive messages meant to manipulate people into following him. Hitler's writing uses an excess of words, with many repetitions of the same basic concepts. This is a tactic of harmful cult groups. In our campus cult, we would use many words but say very little. Propaganda was our friend. The purpose was not to educate or to enlighten, but to persuade active loyalty and obedience.

Confronting our Inner Hitler

Collaboration, teamwork, intercultural activities, coalitions, interdependent relationships—hallmarks of a strong society. Isolationism cuts against this grain, promising some sort of elite strength but always falling short. To say we can "go it alone" is to deny our very humanity. I find such isolation ideology at the heart of Hitler's movement. It was, if nothing else, a movement to promote the German race as the lone supreme race, and Germany as the one great, glorious nation, unparalleled by any other nation and envied by all.

As an independent-minded and introverted person, I see the advantages of individual strength. Having lived for two decades in a personality cult in America, I also see clearly the dire pitfalls of such ideologies. Another man saw these same pitfalls, and reacted strongly against Hitler's isolationist ideas. That man was Dietrich Bonhoeffer.

Bonheoffer's Confessing Church stands out as the primary voice of resistance against Hitler and the Nazi Party. Among many themes that contradicted the Nazi propaganda, the theme of living together remains one of the most enlightened teachings of Bonhoeffer. His book, entitled "Life Together", is a splendid example of how to actually build a powerful society. Such power comes not through living alone, but by living together. It is not surprising then, that isolation is one of the themes Bonhoeffer confronts in his theological writing:

> "*The death and life of Christians are not situated in a self-contained isolation. Rather, Christians encounter both death and life only in the Word that comes to them from the outside, in God's Word to them. The Reformers expressed it by calling our righteousness an "alien righteousness"..., a righteousness that comes from outside of us . . . "*
>
> Dietrich Bonhoeffer
> Life Together & Prayerbook of the Bible

While Hitler promoted the idea that Germany would be strong by being isolated from the rest of the world, Bonhoeffer preached the opposite.

Are we meant to live alone? Are we meant to live in community? Bonhoeffer wrestles with these questions with unmatched brilliance. The answers are not so easy. The solution is not as clear as the Hitlers of the world claim. Human beings are complex creatures. Sometimes we need time alone. Sometimes we need community. One thing is clear however from both Bonhoeffer and Hitler: isolation is evil.

Part Two

WHAT WAS HITLER'S FAITH?

" . . . Hitler suggested a vision of a distant utopia. He did not chart the path to it. But no other Nazi leader or völkisch politician could match the internal unity, simplicity, and all-encompassing character of this 'vision'. His sense of conviction –he spoke frequently of his 'mission', 'faith', and of the 'idea' –combined with an unrivalled talent for mobilization through reduction to simple 'black–white' choices, was where the ideologue and the propagandist came together."

Ian Kershaw, Hitler: A Biography

Mission. Faith. God. These are words Hitler used often. The words riddle his writings. And yet who would claim that Hitler lived a righteous life? If we learn anything from confronting Hitler, we learn that evil does not look like evil in the beginning. In fact evil often looks very much like faith and all the good things in the world. Evil is typically cloaked by what appears to be good. If such were not the case, few would accept the evil. This is the "Trojan horse" nature of evil throughout history. Hitler is no exception.

In this chapter I examine three elements of the faith that cloaked Hitler's evil. In reality, Hitler believed in power, heroic nationalism and extravagant persuasion. His love-less mission, though promoted from the steps of churches, had nothing to do with God, for God is love. We know this now. But could we have known such a thing in 1932, in a time with no internet and in a world filled with war?

The German Jesus

> "To deny the influence of Christianity on Hitler and its role in World War II, means that you must ignore history and forever bar yourself from understanding the source of German anti-Semitism and how the WWII atrocities occurred."
>
> Jim Walker, No Beliefs: Hitler's Christianity

In my study of Hitler and the Nazis the past several years, no writing is more intriguing to me than that of Jim Walker and his website "No Beliefs".[10] Walker has assembled a fascinating collection of quotes and articles that show the evil of mixing politics with religion. My own reading of Hitler and the Nazis leads me to concur with Walker—Hitler created his own brand of Christianity, which historians label as Positive Christianity.[11] I see much value in examining three aspects of this so-called Positive Christianity. Hitler and the Nazi propagandists, such as Joseph Goebbels, created a radical new image of Jesus, fashioned a politicized gospel message, and deceptively misread the Bible.

Jesus. He is central to the Christian faith. Christians, from the beginning of the faith in the first century, have maintained a unique claim. They claim that Jesus is God incarnated—that God walked among us as a man. As such, longstanding Christian theology has asserted that Jesus was fully human, in every way except for sin, and at the same time, fully God. The claim is furthermore that Jesus rose from the dead and is alive and working for good even now.

My point here is not to debate Christianity, but to show how Hitler and his writers co-opted the Christian Jesus and fashioned a German Jesus.

The Nazis created a Jesus who was opposed to the Jews. They created a Jesus who was a hero without a Divine nature. They created a Jesus who was part of the Supreme Race.

Confronting our Inner Hitler

Pause and ponder these words from Hitler himself . . .

"My feelings as a Christian points me to my Lord and Savior as a fighter. It points me to the man who once in loneliness, surrounded by a few followers, recognized these Jews for what they were and summoned men to fight against them and who, God's truth! was greatest not as a sufferer but as a fighter. In boundless love as a Christian and as a man I read through the passage which tells us how the Lord at last rose in His might and seized the scourge to drive out of the Temple the brood of vipers and adders. How terrific was His fight for the world against the Jewish poison. Today, after two thousand years, with deepest emotion I recognize more profoundly than ever before the fact that it was for this that He had to shed His blood upon the Cross.

As a Christian I have no duty to allow myself to be cheated, but I have the duty to be a fighter for truth and justice... And if there is anything which could demonstrate that we are acting rightly it is the distress that daily grows. For as a Christian I have also a duty to my own people."[12]

These are the words Adolf Hitler preached, in a speech on April 12th, 1922.

In Hitler's mind, he was a "fighter for truth and justice". Jesus was not the peace-loving, miracle-working, outcast-helping, always-serving, God-incarnated Anointed One who millions of Christian faithful have adored. Instead, Hitler painted a picture of a Jesus who is a fighter, struggling to start a movement, not unlike Hitler's own struggle.

Hitler saw Jesus as being against the Jews, crusading against the supposed poison of the Jewish religion. Hitler imagined Jesus as a champion of truth and delegator of justice. Hitler zeroed in on the dutiful obedience that he claimed to see in his Jesus.

Hitler and the Nazis painted Jesus as a hero. At times, Hitler confuses himself with the Savoir. Hitler's Jesus becomes a portrayal of Hitler himself. For example, in *Mein Kampf*, Hitler seems to channel Jesus' words:

> *"Verily a man cannot serve two masters. And I consider the foundation or destruction of a religion far greater than the foundation or destruction of a state, let alone a party."* [5]

In the end, Hitler presents a Jesus who is just what he and his movement needs. They need a Jesus who is acceptable enough to appeal to the church-going believers (or at least not offend them too deeply) and who is believable enough to persuade the loyalty of the non-believers.

What Hitler really wants is for the German people to see him as their savior. Hitler becomes a Jesus-figure to the masses, persuading the public to believe that he, and he alone, is their only chance for survival and opportunity as a nation.

Hitler played the religious game masterfully, using religion just as much as he needed to gain political support. The plan worked, as Hitler gained over 13 million votes in the Presidential elections.[8] Hitler came to power by legal appointment and with mass support of the German people. Hitler became the only choice to build a strong new German nation.

The Political Gospel

> *"He was holding the masses, and me with them, under a hypnotic spell by the sheer force of his conviction... His appeal to German manhood was like a call to arms, the gospel he preached a sacred truth. He seemed another Luther... I experienced an exaltation that could be likened only to religious conversion . . . I had found myself, my leader, and my cause."*[14]

Kurt Lüdecke, upon hearing Hitler
at the rally of the Patriotic Associations
in Munich in August 1922

Confronting our Inner Hitler

Every leader needs a message. Every movement needs a mantra. What good news did Hitler and his movement present? I find the answer to be rather vague. Hitler promised many things to many people. The common thread I find in his speeches and in the Nazi party is this: authority to build a nation.

Hitler created his own political gospel. He knew the evil of mixing a religious gospel with politics. So while Hitler certainly used the church's support, he avoided promoting a religious gospel:

> "If in Germany before the War religious life for many had an unpleasant aftertaste, this could be attributed to the abuse of Christianity on the-part of a so-called 'Christian' party and the shameless way in which they attempted to identify the Catholic faith with a political party. This false association was a calamity which may have brought parliamentary mandates to a number of good-for-nothings but injury to the Church."[5]
>
> *Adolph Hitler*

Hitler's gospel, in my observation, is the gospel of authoritarianism. The good news his movement brought was in essence, themselves and their right to build a new nation. The thought was: because we are here and have power, everything will be made right again. Hitler was selling himself. His authority would be the savior of Germany. This is what persuaded men like Kurt Lüdecke to support Hitler and raise money for the Nazi Party. Lüdecke was an ardent German nationalist and successful man with international social connections. Such little-known men were drawn in by Hitler's gospel of authority. Supporting Hitler felt like supporting a glorious new Germany. Whatever plan Hitler and the Nazis had didn't matter at first. What mattered was the idea that they were taking their country back. Men would be men again.

Hitler's gospel has more depth than fascist authoritarianism however. His gospel has a strong vein of racism at its core. Yes he preached authority. More than this however, Hitler preached the gospel of authority inherent in a supreme race—the Aryan race to be exact.

In *Mein Kampf*, Hitler begins a chapter entitled "The State" with these words, announcing his movement's new political gospel:

> "As early as 1920-1921 certain circles belonging to the effete bourgeois class accused our movement again and again of taking up a negative attitude towards the modern State . . . [our opponents tried to suppress] this young movement which was preaching a new political gospel."[5]
>
> *Adolph Hitler*

And then shortly thereafter, Hitler writes out a major tenant of his gospel:

> "What makes a people or, to be more correct, a race, is not language but blood."[5]

Hitler goes on to define his idea of the State, how the supreme German race, bound by what he called German blood, has the right to exist in a pure state. Those who would blemish this blood, who were not of the German race, were to be eliminated. Hitler saw non-Germans, who did not speak German natively, as evil.

We Americans now must ask ourselves this very question: What makes a people? What makes us Americans? How do we treat those who do not speak English? What do we do to those who dress differently from us or admire a different sacred text than the Bible?

Might we see the evil in Hitler's answers to these questions? Do we identify a supreme race and exterminate those who do not fit? Is our faith in authority and power to form a great nation? Are we desperate to rid our country of those who do not speak English? If these are the essence of our gospel, then

Confronting our Inner Hitler

we have already fallen into the evil found in Hitler's political gospel.

The Nazi Bible

> *"Their sword will become our plow, and from the tears of war the daily bread of future generations will grow."*[5]
>
> Adolf Hitler

Hitler, at times, writes as if he is the Holy One speaking Scripture. Is he quoting Joel 3:9-10 from the Bible? Or is he making up new teachings? He peppers his words and speeches with Biblical-sounding words. In doing so, he sounds humble and God-fearing at times. Perhaps this helped his appeal with the church-going folks. In any case, Hitler and his movement not only fashioned a new Jesus and a new Gospel, but also a new Bible.

As I survey some of the words from Nazi Party leaders, I am shocked to find numerous references to the Bible. Let's pause for a moment and realize the evil here . . .

Joseph Goebbels claimed to read the Sermon on the Mount all day long:

> *"I take the Bible, and all evening long I read the simplest and greatest sermon that has ever been given to mankind: The Sermon on the Mount! 'Blessed are they who suffer persecution for the sake of justice, for theirs is the kingdom of heaven'"!* [15]

Hans Schemm marveled at Martin Luther's contribution to the German people regarding the Bible:

> *"When Luther made the Bible accessible to Germans in the glorious German language, it was as if we had cast off the iron glove and with the flesh and blood of our German hand were finally able to grasp our unique character . . ."* [15]

EVIL

Helmut Brucker expressed the Nazi Party's desire for a united church, entangling the threads of faith, politics and ideology into a unified concept:

> *"We struggle for a union of the small Protestant state churches into a strong Protestant Reich Church.... We are acting not as a party, but as Protestant Christians who only follow a call to faith from God, which we here in our Volk movement. As true members of our church we have a legitimate claim to have appropriate consideration given to the greatness and inner strength of National Socialism in church life and the church administration."*[15]

Many more examples of the mixing of the Bible and the courting of the Protestant churches exist in Nazi speeches and in Hitler's own writing. Can we discern a people of God from people of evil? Do we know the Bible well enough to expose charlatans who would sway the church?

Part Three

CONFRONTING EVIL

"If only it were all so simple! If only there were evil people somewhere insidiously committing evil deeds, and it were necessary only to separate them from the rest of us and destroy them. But the line dividing good and evil cuts through the heart of every human being. And who is willing to destroy a piece of his own heart?"

Aleksandr Solzhenitsyn
The Gulag Archipelago 1918-1956

If humanity is a mixture of good and evil, how do we go about confronting evil? Such a task is not as simple as cultic and fascist leaders would have us believe. The Hitlers of the world tell us so clearly what and who evil is, and how to remove it. Always the Hitlers of the world say evil is in "the other". Rather than looking to confront other people's evil, I suggest we take a moment to look inward. I am in no way suggesting we remain there, staring into the mirror of narcissism. I am pleading with you, however, to begin with confronting your own evil. Are you willing to constrain the evil in your own heart?

As a survivor of a Korean mind-control cult, I find such a task highly challenging. The evil seems so clear to me. I am convinced I know who the evil people are and who must be held accountable—*those Korean leaders of my former group!* How I have, at times, longed for the "fire from Heaven" to destroy my former cult group, ridding the earth of their stench. Alas, this is the evil in my own heart. The leaders in the group are no more evil than myself. And yet something in me calls out, almost pushing me onward to confront the evil of those who would abuse children, take advantage of college students, gather up large sums of money, and pretend they are the God-ordained shepherds for the world. Such evil must be confronted. But how can this be done without fueling the evil in my own heart?

Given my Christian faith, I turn to the words of Jesus himself. When I study Jesus' teachings, I find my path—the way to confront evil without falling into greater evil myself. I find the strength to expose my former cult group's harmful ideology and abusive practices without becoming lost in bitter hatred.

I find such a path so very relevant in confronting the evil I find in the 1930's Hitler and Nazi generation. The key is somewhat ironic—the path out of evil lies not in confronting the leaders but in confronting the followers. Are not those who enable and support at the root of the problem? There will always be evil people who take advantage of others. Such evil, however, is rendered impotent by the fascinating power of love. All the terror of the Third Reich failed to impact my life with evil. All the abuse of the Bible cult group could not control my life forever. I escaped their control and stopped enabling their influence over my family's lives. Why? The reason is because of my Grandparents' love. They chose the humble path of love, and that love continues to be a bedrock of goodness for me and the rest of our family. Their love broke the chains of evil control the Korean Bible cult held over my life. It is love that frees us—love for our enemy, our stranger, our family, our neighbor, our outcast. Can we love the "other"?

In this chapter I turn now to Jesus' words in the Bible, in Matthew 23 to be exact. Here Jesus speaks with righteous indignation, calling out seven evils. If you hear only an anti-Jewish or anti-religion message in Jesus' words, your theology is no better than Hitler; you have missed Jesus' point entirely. In Matthew 23, Jesus confronts seven evils and shows us seven specific kinds of love. This then, is the path to walk, the path of confronting evil with love.

Confronting our Inner Hitler

What is Evil?

So, so you think you can tell . . .
Heaven from Hell
Blue skies from pain
Can you tell a green field from a cold steel rail?
A smile from a veil?
Do you think you can tell?

Pink Floyd, Wish You Were Here

In all the religions, philosophies and artistic expressions of humanity throughout the ages, no one has succeeded in removing evil from the hearts of people. Evil continues. Attempts to eradicate evil continue to fail. In the end, those who learn to accept this age-old reality are those who succeed in giving the world a bit more goodness in spite of evil. Such people are those like my Grandparents, who sought the goodness of love and family in the midst of Hitler's savagery.

The major religions all accept this reality—humanity is a mixture of good and evil, and has the ability to choose between them. Though it may be difficult to discern good from evil, we have the ability to do so. Evil exists, but evil can be overcome with good.

Jesus said, "If you then, who are evil, know how to give good gifts to your children, how much more will the heavenly Father give the Holy Spirit to those who ask him!" (Luke 11:13 ESV Bible). Islam expresses humanity as having both "the consciousness of evil and piety" (Quran, Surah Ash-Shams 91:8). Hindu sages speak volumes about the good and evil of humanity. For example, "We may or may not understand it, but the results of our acts are always mixed with good and evil." (Swami Abhedananda Ramakrishna Vedanta Math).

Judaism is also rife with this line of thought. Many rabbis expound on both the evil inclination and the good inclination embedded in human beings. For example, Moshe Chaim Luzzatto, a prominent Italian Jewish rabbi, wrote in Derech

Hashem ("The Way of God") the following thought: "Man's inclinations are balanced between good (Yetzer HaTov) and evil (Yetzer HaRa), and he is not compelled toward either of them. He has the power of choice and is able to choose either side knowingly and willingly . . . "

It is with this starting point, this universal common ground, often called the "golden rule", which I begin. Every religion says it, though slightly differently: *treat others the way you want to be treated*. While we may never be able to fully separate good from evil, we have the ability to confront evil and to seek good. Ideologies that teach otherwise are but glass menagerie constructs that repeatedly shatter on the rock of reality. To teach that humanity has no control over good and evil is to surrender to evil itself. To say that human beings are only good is to live in ignorance. To claim that human beings are incapable of choosing good is to live in slavery to fear. Evil exists. Good exists. To live in peace, we therefore are compelled to confront evil and promote good.

Black and white . . . Good and evil . . . Us versus them . . . I am all for clarity yet binary thinking rarely clarifies anything about humanity. Analog perspectives often do far more in exposing the clarity we seek. Humanity is not as simple as male and female or conservative and liberal. Human beings are massively complex on one level, and at the same time simplistic animals on another level. We are evil, and yet we know how to do good.

The Evil of Exclusion

> *"But woe to you, scribes and Pharisees, hypocrites! For you shut the kingdom of heaven in people's faces. For you neither enter yourselves nor allow those who would enter to go in."*
>
> Jesus of Nazareth, Matthew 23:13 ESV

Hitler's solution to the worldview problem was to create another worldview, but one with power and authority. Hitler's

Confronting our Inner Hitler

final solution to the problem of evil is to convert, exclude, and destroy those who opposed his worldview.

Are we any different? Today in America I see the door to churches being shut in people's faces. The door to freedom is being slammed shut as we batten down the hatches of our country.

The dangerous trend in America that I see is not the erosion of morality, but the building of walls. We have excluded the other—the other race, the other gender, the other religion, and the other person who does not fit in with our worldview. The great melting pot has solidified and cracked into pieces. We now gather together according to our tribes. The fire of inclusion has gone out in America. Until we light such a fire again, we risk losing the unity that America stands for.

The Evil of Ideological Conversion

> *"Woe to you, scribes and Pharisees, hypocrites! For you travel across sea and land to make a single proselyte, and when he becomes a proselyte, you make him twice as much a child of hell as yourselves."*
>
> Jesus of Nazareth, Matthew 23:15 ESV

A proselyte is a person who has converted from one opinion, religion, or party to another, especially recently. American Protestant Christianity thrives on proselytes. In fact, if no one converted to American Protestantism it would die off. Is that the church Jesus promised to build? Clearly not. Jesus is saying here that recruiting converts to our worldview is evil. He is telling us that conversion is not the discipleship he has in mind.

I suppose someone just threw this book against the wall and shouted how can that be? Christianity is all about making converts! I challenge this notion and suggest to you that such conversion is evil. I turn to Bonhoeffer for an explanation.

Bonheoffer speaks of emotional conversion, an experience that is not genuine or lasting. Bonheoffer is not saying that emotions are to be denied or neglected or that conversion experiences themselves are evil, but rather pointing out that genuine conversion to goodness, in the Christian sense, has nothing to do with an emotional appeal to human ideology. Christian conversion has everything to do with an encounter with the Divine forgiveness and a surrendering of our pride to love.

In contrast to ideological conversion, Bonheoffer writes about confessional conversion. He writes repeatedly that "confession is conversion".[13] Thus Bonheoffer agrees with Jesus. Recruitment of converts is evil; confessional conversion in light of a religious experience is good.

In stark contrast to both Jesus and Bonheoffer, Hitler speaks of converting to a new worldview and ideological constructs that center on racial definitions and roles.

Might we pause here and consider one of great root causes of the decline of the institutional churches in America? I suggest that the church in America, especially the Protestant churches who have been fragmented into uncountable factions, have declined because we have upheld the evil of making converts as our gospel. The assembly line is awesome for making cars; it is evil when making disciples.

The Evil of Sacred Separation

> *"Woe to you, blind guides, who say, 'If anyone swears by the temple, it is nothing, but if anyone swears by the gold of the temple, he is bound by his oath.' You blind fools! For which is greater, the gold or the temple that has made the gold sacred?"*
>
> Jesus of Nazareth, Matthew 23:16-17 ESV

In Jesus' time, a growing number of people separated the sacred from the secular. Naturally, the value of the sacred things, such as the Temple, decreased. What mattered to many

Confronting our Inner Hitler

was gold. Those who had gold were included in worship and other activities. Those who did not have gold were excluded. Instead of seeing the sacredness of community which included the "other", gold began to divide the people.

In my observation, the melting pot that America once was, has solidified. The fire of inclusion of the "other" has gone out. Instead of saying to the world "Give me your huddled masses . . . ", we say "Go away . . . unless you have gold." We have separated into diametrically opposed camps: Republican vs Democrat, conservative vs liberal, pro-life vs pro-choice, black vs white, poor vs rich—and the list goes on and on. We have forgotten how much we need each other. We have lost the sacredness of community.

At the root of all this is something I call sacred separation. Such separation is evil. We have de-friended our once friends and even family members. We have quoted Bible verses justifying our worldviews and refused to intelligently discuss the very questions that would lead us to resolutions. We have separated the world into a great sacred vs secular divide.

We each cling our sacred cows—the things we swear by. In Jesus' time, people were dividing. Those who swore by the temple separated from those who swore by the gold in the temple. Those who swore by the gold held the oaths binding only if the gold was involved. Other oaths were arbitrary. This division of what is considered sacred is a most dangerous kind of evil.

Even Hitler knew this. I find it supremely ironic that Hitler, the face of evil, issues a dire warning that American Christianity ought to heed. That's right, I am proposing that the church in America take advice from Hitler. Even though Hitler's solutions are another kind of evil, he did correctly point out one of the greatest evils in the world: religious division.

In Mein Kampf, Hitler wrote:

> " . . . the Jew has attained the ends he desired. Catholics and Protestants are fighting with one another to their

EVIL

hearts' content, while the enemy of Aryan humanity and all Christendom is laughing up his sleeve."[5]

Hitler laughed as the church divided along the fault point of Luther's nail:

> "The two Christian denominations look on with indifference at the profanation and destruction of a noble and unique creature who was given to the world as a gift of God's grace. For the future of the world, however, it does not matter which of the two triumphs over the other, the Catholic or the Protestant. But it does matter whether Aryan humanity survives or perishes. And yet the two Christian denominations are not contending against the destroyer of Aryan humanity but are trying to destroy one another."[5]

Putting aside Hitler's racist remarks, can you hear Hitler's warning? Is evil laughing as we Christians divide ourselves? Might we see the sacredness of all human beings?

The Evil of Piety Without Mercy

> "Woe to you, scribes and Pharisees, hypocrites! For you tithe mint and dill and cumin, and have neglected the weightier matters of the law: justice and mercy and faithfulness. These you ought to have done, without neglecting the others. You blind guides, straining out a gnat and swallowing a camel!"
>
> *Jesus of Nazareth, Matthew 23:23-24 ESV*

Again I turn to Hitler for a second warning that American Christianity needs to ponder. In addition to the good the Christianity has brought to the world, the Christian religion has also brought spiritual terror to the world. Hitler rightly points this out:

> "Each one of us today may regret the fact that the advent of Christianity was the first occasion on which spiritual terror was introduced into the much freer ancient world, but the fact cannot be denied that ever since then the world

Confronting our Inner Hitler

is pervaded and dominated by this kind of coercion . . ."[5]

Adolph Hitler

The Christian religion has often departed from the path Jesus of Nazareth intended. The very purpose of Jesus was liberation and yet in his name, many have introduced forceful domination and spiritual terror. Many preachers in America have presented the psychotic, wrathful God who kills his enemies with blood-thirsty joy. Only those who convert to a hell-centric theology will be saved, they preach. Instead of love and peace uniting our churches, spiritual terror has wreaked havoc among us.

My term for such terror is piety without mercy. Mercy is a dominate theme of Jesus' teachings and yet how quickly we forget to temper our justice with mercy!

The Evil of Double Standards

"Woe to you, scribes and Pharisees, hypocrites! For you clean the outside of the cup and the plate, but inside they are full of greed and self-indulgence."

Jesus of Nazareth, Matthew 23:25 ESV

Double standards. We witness high-profile examples almost daily in America, especially in the church. Those who condemn the gender and sexual minorities among us seem most prone to come out as gay themselves. Those who preach the moral high ground so often seem to be the first to fall. Those who rail against violence seem to be the first to take up arms. Those who seek to be inclusive seem to so quickly seek to exclude. Might we confront the evil in our own hearts?

Hypocrisy is the epitome of evil. And yet we human beings have the ability to confront such hypocrisy and remove its sting in our lives.

As a social media user, I am of course inundated with memes. Most are harmless fun. Some are poignant examples of reality. Others are just downright hilarious! One meme that disturbs me to no end however is the Christian meme that says this: "I am a hypocrite, but God loves me anyway." I find this a disgusting example of evil. Surely hypocrisy lives in all of us. Just as surely however, hypocrisy can be overcome.

Here again Jesus has an answer. The answer is repentance. Yes we all stumble with hypocrisy. The way to overcome it is to change our mindset: we strive to learn from other people, listen to criticism and in the end, simply admit we have failed. To blindly enforce double-standards in order to protect our pride is a terrible evil that is destroying the church in America. Admit it. We failed. Our gospel is flawed. Our movement is arrogant.

The Evil of Religious Pride

> *"Woe to you, scribes and Pharisees, hypocrites! For you are like whitewashed tombs, which outwardly appear beautiful, but within are full of dead people's bones and all uncleanness."*
>
> *Jesus of Nazareth, Matthew 23:27 ESV*

The harshest words of Jesus are reserved for the religious leaders. Embedded in these condemnations are also the kindest words of all—the way to overcome evil with good. By pointing out the flaws of the religious leaders, Jesus was not promoting his religion at the expense of the Jewish religion. Instead, Jesus was showing love by exposing the flaws and pointing to a better way forward.

I find religious pride to be deeply rooted in the American church. We have become proud of our religion, becoming blind to our religious sins. We are quick to condemn moral failures in others and act as if our sins are better. We have grouped sin into to broad categories—those "wild living" moral sins that are to be condemned and those "not so bad" relationship sins that are to be overlooked. This is precisely

Confronting our Inner Hitler

the condition Jesus exposes in his parable about the prodigal son.

In the bible's parable of the prodigal son, found in Luke 15:11-32, the younger of the two brothers squanders his father's wealth in wild living. The older of the two brothers stays at home and strives to obey his father. In the end, the younger brother returns home and his father celebrates, welcoming his wayward son with open arms and a feast fit for a king. The older brother is offended by his father's forgiveness toward his younger brother. So the thought occurred to me—What if God chose to welcome all people (yes even "those" people) just the same—with no conditions like the father in Jesus' parable?

Somehow the church has gotten the idea that this parable indicates two lifestyles and that the sin of wild living is the worse lifestyle. We excuse ourselves just like the older brother and fail to see that this parable is not so much about two different lifestyles but about the father's love for both sons. We've given the world this message: Younger brother sins, such as wild living, are unacceptable and should be condemned, but older brother sins, such as arrogance or hypocrisy, are forgivable and should be tolerated. This entanglement is a most unfortunate stumbling block for everyone.

The thought may be that the older brother at least tried to obey his father, please his parents and keep his life clean. So if we avoid "wild living" or "grave sins", we are somehow right with God. Many preachers then let the older brother off the hook in some form. And yet it is repeatedly seen in the bible that God is far more angered by the arrogance, pride, exclusiveness and uncaring nature of the older brother in Jesus' parable.

One unmistakable teaching of Jesus and his parables is this: religious pride is evil.

EVIL

The Evil of Violence

> *"Woe to you, scribes and Pharisees, hypocrites! For you build the tombs of the prophets and decorate the monuments of the righteous, saying, 'If we had lived in the days of our fathers, we would not have taken part with them in shedding the blood of the prophets.' Thus you witness against yourselves that you are sons of those who murdered the prophets. Fill up, then, the measure of your fathers. You serpents, you brood of vipers, how are you to escape being sentenced to hell?"*
>
> Jesus of Nazareth, Matthew 23:29-33 ESV

If there was one definition of evil that people could agree on, I would think that violence would be that definition. In the church, where love and peace are supposed to be supreme values, could we not agree that violence is evil? It seems self-explanatory to me. Sadly, it is not. In fact, many of the greatest atrocities in history, Hitler's included, were done either by the church directly or enacted by others while the church watched in silence. The forces of good in the church have at times been used for absurd acts of violence.

The violence against Martin Luther King, Jr., for example, stands as a glaring example of such evil. Why would someone murder such a good man? King's words ring true forevermore:

> *"The ultimate weakness of violence is that it is a descending spiral; begetting the very thing it seeks to destroy. Instead of diminishing evil, it multiplies it. Through violence you may murder the liar, but you cannot murder the lie, nor establish the truth. Through violence you may murder the hater, but you do not murder hate. In fact, violence merely increases hate."*
>
> Martin Luther King, Jr.,
Where Do We Go from Here:
Chaos or Community?

Confronting our Inner Hitler

I have observed that the church has promoted an image of the "new believer" in Christ as a sort of violent, man-up type image masked by the pretense of peace. Our preachers paint pictures of ideal Christians as people who are truth fighters and justice defenders. When did the image of love for the outcast disappear from the church? We all seem to be encouraged to act peacefully, wearing a "happy mask" if necessary, and to keep all our real thoughts to ourselves. We pretend to love while harboring violent thoughts in our souls.

When this caricature of Christian life meets the social networks, we see an explosion of vitriol, endless arguments and a chaotic mess that lacks civility and drags philosophical debate into oblivion. It may be that because the internet has given us anonymity, we are allowed to keep our church mask on as we spew our violent hearts, all with little consequence, other than the occasional de-friending. I believe the advent of the internet and social media has revealed the church's flawed, violent self-image in glorious fashion. Our true, inner fruit has been born, and it is not good.

Part Four

LAMENT + **HOPE**

> "O Jerusalem, Jerusalem, the city that kills the prophets and stones those who are sent to it! How often would I have gathered your children together as a hen gathers her brood under her wings, and you were not willing! See, your house is left to you desolate. For I tell you, you will not see me again, until you say, 'Blessed is he who comes in the name of the Lord.'"
>
> Jesus Christ, Matthew 23:37-39 ESV

Pride. It is a tough pill to swallow. To admit that I am wrong, to question my worldview, to consider the possibility that I just don't have all the answers for the evils of the world—this is the moment of transformation. Such a moment is the fulcrum of the change we seek. The moment we stop berating the other and surrender our pride, that is the moment of contentment.

God had such a moment, according to the Biblical passages. The way of religion had always been a way of sacrifice. The gods demanded sacrifice and even God demanded sacrifice. Justice had to be served. The holy codes had to be followed. Righteousness must be preserved and the truth protected. And then Jesus was born.

In the life, ministry and death of Jesus of Nazareth I see God's surrender. Evil exists in the world. Until the end of days, evil will grow with good. The Hitlers of the world will always be born and rise to power. The solution to evil, as I see it, is to encourage the rise of the Bonheoffers of the world. Evil is rendered impotent when we the people choose surrender over pride. In 1932 Germany, there was only one Bonheoffer. This world will be far more safe when there are more who rise up to resist evil with good and overcome fear with love. As long as we are bent on destroying our enemies, the cycle of evil will continue.

Living Together

> *"Living together is an art. It's a patient art, it's a beautiful art, it's fascinating."*
>
> Pope Francis, February 14, 2014

It's a small world after all. Our neighbor around the world is instantly accessible. How can we learn to live together? Our world today is smaller in that we are more inter-connected and inter-dependent than at any time in world history. Instant, global communication and rapid world-wide travel is commonplace.

The worldwide Christian church is starting to realize that there is only one faith, one hope, one Lord and one body. Our theologies and gospel messages must now pass the test of global criticism. Perhaps we are on the verge of a new kind of uniting by the Holy Spirit that does not define boundaries? Clearly church communities have been ripped to shreds in recent years. Could the Spirit now be uniting entirely new communities, reforming the shattered body of Christ into a vastly more healthy and loving world-wide community?

Here in America, we have atomized and democratized everything from religion to pizza. I have the world at my laptop, and so do you. Some do not yet have this, but in time the atomization will reach critical mass. The new question is: how can we communalize in a healthy manner? How can we learn to live together in an atomized, systemized world?

In Russia, the ideal social construct is to communalize the world. In America, the ideal social construct is to democratize

Confronting our Inner Hitler

the world. History teaches us, especially 1930's German history, that exerting our particular social construct on the world by force leads to disastrous results. We must confront the fact that Americans simply will not be able to democratize the world. At some point, we must stop and consider how to build safe communities. Only by communities that can live in peace with each other's diversity can the world become a better place. As long as we attempt to protect and impose our ideal social constructs and worldviews on others, revolution and war will continue.

Resisting Evil

> *"Merely to resist evil with evil by hating those who hate us and seeking to destroy them, is actually no resistance at all. It is active and purposeful collaboration in evil that brings the Christian into direct and intimate contact with the same source of evil and hatred which inspires the acts of his enemy. It leads in practice to a denial of Christ and to the service of hatred rather than love."*
>
> Thomas Merton, Passion for Peace;
Reflections on War and Nonviolence

Every kindergarten teacher knows this basic premise: resisting evil is not done with more evil. If one child fights with another child, the solution is not to urge all the students to fight with each other! The solution is to show them a better way—the way of love.

Sometimes though, evil seems overwhelming. The violence pours from our streets. Even the police are sometimes swayed into violence. What can be done?

Never underestimate the impact one person can have. For example, in 1842 an artist was commissioned to paint a series of paintings. The result was Thomas Cole's four paintings entitled "The Voyage of Life". If paintings were sermons, I might call this the Sermon on the Mount! These four paintings tell the magnificent story of human life from childhood, youth, manhood and old age. Over 170 years later, these paintings still invoke marvel and awe—and such overwhelming goodness.

My wife and I had a copy of these paintings on a wall in our first house. Recalling all the events that transpired the past several years sometimes leaves me feeling detached and alone. What was it all for? The answer is love. We are never alone when we have love. Thomas Cole's paintings remind me that love is both constant and maturing as we progress through the stages of life. His Voyage paintings inspire me to believe that each of us has an epic life to live.

I once pursued an epic life by imagining I was a holy soldier, fighting to remove evil in the world. Me and the others in our isolated Bible cult believed we had found the cure for all ills in society. We were the people supposedly charged by God to make America a "kingdom of priests and a holy nation". We thought that if everyone would just be holy, like a priest, all would be well. That wish dream shattered as reality stepped in. As my wife and I left the cult group, I felt overwhelmed by deceptive evil.

How could I have been so blind to have supported a group where leaders abused people continually and called it "holy training"? Will I ever want to read the bible or believe in God again? Those questions stuck in my mind every day for quite some time. I simply could not read the bible. And I didn't want anything to do with church or religion. Too many post-traumatic-stress-like reactions kept happening if I happened to read a bible verse or attend a church service. I could not stand seeing those pretty Facebook memes with bible verses on them!

Then I discovered The Message paraphrase and the ESV bible translation. I discovered some real gems in The Message. Take this reading of Psalm 73:11-14 for example: "What's going on here? Is God out to lunch? Nobody's tending the store. The wicked get by with everything; they have it made, piling up riches. I've been stupid to play by the rules; what

Confronting our Inner Hitler

has it gotten me? A long run of bad luck, that's what—a slap in the face every time I walk out the door."

And suddenly the bible seemed interesting again. All at once I found a remarkable way to confront evil, not by removing abusive leaders, but by resisting them.

Forgiving Our Enemies

> *"Some have traditionally interpreted the idea of loving one's enemies in the narrow sense of love for one's own tribe or private community . . . Such an interpretation, however, keeps us from coming into the fullness of the gospel and being made evermore into God's likeness. Indeed, Jesus tells us in the very next line that the reason we are to love our enemies is so that we might be like God himself (see Matthew 5:45), one who loves both the righteous and unrighteous and blesses those who are evil as well as those who are good. Luke's Gospel tells us that "he is kind to the ungrateful and the wicked."*
>
> *James Danaher, Eyes That See, Ears That Hear: Perceiving Jesus in a Postmodern Context*

What do people want? People want to be known, to be accepted, to be happy, to be safe and to be free from danger or threat. I find that behind all this, we often also want forgiveness. If we want these things, might we consider that our enemy also wants these very same things?

The question that has disturbed my mind is this: Will God forgive his enemies? Clearly the God of the bible expects his people to forgive their enemies as we read in the text containing Matthew 5:44, Matthew 18:35, Luke 6:35 and many other places in the bible. If God expects me to forgive my enemies, will not God do so as well? This is a complex issue to ponder.

In our post-post-modern world, many have pointed out the hell-bent, angry, nearly narcissistic God portrayed in the bible texts. Is this wrathful God of retribution the only picture of

EVIL

God? Are we to be left with fear? If there is anything Christian in me, I can say without a doubt, certainly not! Surely we see a deeper vision of God in the bible. Surely we can have eyes to see beyond the wrath of God and see the good purposes of God? Where do we look to find such deeper truths?

I look now at the cross. The cross is something that is at the same time ugly and ghastly and beautiful and astounding. On the cross, Jesus was surrounded by his enemies. One could argue that all humanity was Jesus' enemy that fateful day. What did Jesus do in that situation, being surrounded by enemies? One thing Jesus did was to pray, "Father, forgive them."

Much has been written about the cross and these famous words of Jesus. I will not delve into the deep meanings that others have expounded on with eloquence. I could not do the words justice. I can however notice something rather odd. Jesus did not say "I forgive them". Jesus said, "Father, forgive them." Could this be Jesus giving us a great example of what we humans can do when we have no strength or ability in us to forgive? What can we do when we cannot forgive those who have abused us, those who have harmed us, those who have mistreated us? What can we do when we cannot forgive the church, or maintain fellowship with the people who claim to know God because they have failed us? Jesus shows us the way. When we cannot say "I forgive them" we can pray "Father, forgive them".

What if God forgives his enemies? Will God do this? Will God answer Jesus' cross-originated prayer to forgive his enemies, God's enemies? Could there be forgiveness beyond the judgment of God? How might the enemies of God find the forgiveness of God? As I searched the bible feverishly and prayed for answers to such questions, I didn't find all the answers. But I did find someone who wrestled with these kinds of questions. His name was Paul the Apostle.

In Romans chapter 9, he wrestles with such questions: What if God, choosing to show his wrath and make his power known, bore with great patience the objects of his wrath--

prepared for destruction? What if he did this to make the riches of his glory known to the objects of his mercy, whom he prepared in advance for glory-- even us, whom he also called, not only from the Jews but also from the Gentiles? (Romans 9:22-24)

The Gentiles!? How could the God of Abraham bear with Gentiles? The most infamous of the Gentiles are the Edomites! Esau might be called a patriarch of the Gentiles, the grandfather of wickedness. Would God bear with them? Would God reveal the riches of his glory through those people? They are violent and ungodly. Would God even go so far as to call Gentiles to be part of his kingdom? Could Gentiles become Christians?

Paul the Apostle finds answers in the prophet Hosea, discerning that God's new purpose of love and forgiveness for all of humanity, both Jews and Gentiles, found on the cross, is rooted in God's old purpose, as foretold by Hosea. To Paul's surprise, he finds that such love and forgiveness of the God of Abraham is rooted in both the objects of God's wrath and the objects of God's mercy, that all may be one. In the place where it was said to them, "You are not my people," it shall be said to them, "Children of the living God."

The Edomites, the enemies of God, are shown by God no mercy in the biblical texts. And yet what does Paul discern about such enemies? God will have mercy on "No Mercy". God will say to "Not My People", "You are my people" (Hosea 1:1-11; Hosea 2:1-23; Romans 5:1-21; Romans 9:1-33). I believe this grand vision of ultimate forgiveness opens our eyes to begin to see the cosmic redemption narrative of the God of Abraham, and the interconnected nature of all three Abrahamic faiths.

In the end I am filled with both lament and hope. The perfect storm of politics, religion and economics is at hand. Will 2016 America fare any better than 1932 Germany?

REFERENCES

1. "Sure, call Trump a Nazi. Just make sure you know what you're talking about" https://www.washingtonpost.com/posteverything/wp/2015/12/14/sure-call-trump-a-nazi-just-make-sure-you-know-what-youre-talking-about/?postshare=4271450186360203&tid=ss_tw

2. "'Mein Kampf' to be republished in Germany 70 years after Hitler's death", http://www.cnn.com/2015/12/02/europe/germany-mein-kampf-republication-annotated/index.html

3. "Hitler, Mein Kampf. A critical edition", http://www.ifz-muenchen.de/?id=550

4. Godwin, Mike (October 1994). "Meme, Counter-meme". Wired. Retrieved March 24, 2006.

5. Mein Kampf, by Adolf Hitler, The Noontide Press: Books On-Line

6. "Beer hall Putsch", https://en.wikipedia.org/wiki/Beer_Hall_Putsch

7. "The Rise of Hitler", http://www.historyplace.com/worldwar2/riseofhitler/runs.htm Copyright © 1996 The History Place™ All Rights Reserved, Philip Gavin, Bachelor of Arts, Northeastern University; Master of Science, Boston University.

8. Kolb, Eberhard (2005) [1984], The Weimar Republic, London; New York: Routledge, ISBN 978-0-415-34441-8.

9. BBC Bitesize, "The rise of the Nazi Party and its consolidation of power"http://www.bbc.co.uk/schools/gcsebitesize/history/tch_wjec/germany19291947/1hitlerchancellor3.shtml

10. "No Beliefs: Hitler's Christianity", Jim Walker, http://www.nobeliefs.com/Hitler1.htm

11. NSDAP Party Program. 24 February 1920, Point 24: "We demand freedom of religion for all religious denominations within the state so long as they do not endanger its existence or oppose the moral senses of the Germanic race. The Party as such advocates the standpoint of a positive Christianity without binding itself confessionally to any one denomination.", Robert Michael; Philip Rosen (2007). Dictionary of Antisemitism from the Earliest Times to the Present. Lanham: Scarecrow Press. p. 321.

12. Norman H. Baynes, ed. The Speeches of Adolf Hitler, April 1922-August 1939, Vol. 1 of 2, pp. 19-20, Oxford University Press, 1942.

13. Dietrich Bonhoeffer, Life Together and the Prayer Book of the Bible, Kindle Edition.

14. Ian Kershaw, Hitler: A Biography, Kindle Edition.

15. Richard Steigmann-Gall, The Holy Reich

16. Lauteinann, Geschichten in Quellen Bd. 6, S. 129, https://en.wikipedia.org/wiki/Treaty_of_Versailles

ABOUT THE AUTHOR

Brian John Karcher
author · architect · ally

Intentionally discussing taboo topics with clarity . . .

Brian is an almost priest, an almost missionary and an almost pastor. He is a Christ-follower on the journey of life who loves family, friends, philosophy, writing, blogging and dialogue. He loves all things related to Steelers, technology and penguins. He has been happily married to a wonderful, intelligent and beautiful wife since 1994 and has four amazing children.

Brian's religious background is extensive. He grew up in the Roman Catholic Church, participating in Catechism classes through high school as well as completing the sacraments of Baptism, Confirmation and First Communion. In college he became a leader in a campus bible study organization from Korea where he donated nearly 40 hours of time every week for 16 years. He has gone to Russia as a missionary, amassed over 15,000 hours of bible meditation and was pastor in his own house church for eight years. Currently he does not attend any church and considers himself one of the "dones."

YACOB & TOMAS

www.ingramcontent.com/pod-product-compliance
Lightning Source LLC
Chambersburg PA
CBHW020623300426
44113CB00007B/756